Martin Luther King Jr.

Dare To Dream

The True Story of an Civil Rights
Icon

Anna Revell

Table of Contents

Introduction

There is no way to talk about the history of the United States of America without talking about the history of the African American men and women who have inhabited this great country since before it was founded. Unfortunately, the relationship between the races in the U.S. has never recovered from the centuries of slavery that the African Americans were subjected to by their European counterparts.

Yet, there has been progress throughout the years. It's possible that, eventually, the past will fall away and reveal a future of peaceful cohabitation. If that ever happens, there is one man that the world will look to as the father of the Civil Rights Movement: Martin Luther King Jr.

Not only was Martin Luther King responsible for some of the most dramatic political opposition to segregation and racism, he is the reason that civil disobedience was the main tool of the Civil Rights Movement. King was a pacifist and urged his followers to follow suit. He was able to gather the courage to do this by studying the ways of the indomitable Mahatma Gandhi and the incredible victories achievable by using only peaceful techniques.

King hoped to bring the success that the Indian people had found to America. He found many similarities between the way

African Americans were treated in the United States and the "untouchable" caste of India.

His other main influence was Henry David Thoreau, who quite literally wrote the book on Civil Disobedience in the 1800's. Thoreau would protest through peaceable actions that disrupted the every-day business of a community. King believed that was the best option available, knowing that the world he wished to live in would be one that included all races of people.

King believed that racism and segregation were an affront to God, himself. He knew that all people are equal under the eyes of God and fought for it. King would often cite the constitution's assertion that all men are created equal and tried desperately to get his country to follow suit.

King was a deeply religious man and used the power of religion in the South (and America in general) to appeal to the goodness in all people. He spoke as a reverend and many felt that his words reverberated with divine power. However, it could also be that King was extensively educated and revered the great speakers of equality and rights throughout history.

Yet, he was always surrounded by enemies that would work for years to undermine his efforts and his life. The attacks and humiliation heaped upon him and his friends and family are beyond this author's understanding. Over the years, the multitude of threats would include death to his family, property, and reputation. Many still believe that the government of the time had a hand in some of the violence committed.

It is true that the police brutality of the era is beyond anything that the modern American can understand. The institutional support of the United States was firmly in support of segregation and operated on the basis of racial tenets that were embedded in both the North and the South since far before the Civil War.

However, the United States government took it one step further, accusing King of Communism and surveilling him constantly once it became clear that he was at the forefront to a movement that they had no control of. The FBI was at the forefront of this and was known, at the time, for violating human rights and decency even if it was a high-profile character like Martin Luther King Jr. and even John Lennon.

They would be on the wrong side of history. What they didn't count on was the power of King's actions living on far longer than his body could take them. He lived in a time that was capable of preserving images and words in a clear enough way to pass them down for generations. Over the years, people of all races have come to respect him as an American hero.

This reaction is less than miraculous, in fact, it's predictable. King was a legendary speaker and held crowds, numbering in the thousands, in silence as he spoke about the struggle of the African American cause. Not only that, but the marches he organized are some of the most popular and effective marches in American history, immortalized by the famous March on Washington in which King spoke to a crowd of more than 200,000 American citizens.

When King felt that he had made as much progress as possible using the message made popular during the heyday of the Civil Rights Movement, he went and created another organization known as the Poor People's Campaign. He considered the plight of the poor and disenfranchised to be indelibly connected to that of African Americans.

However, during the planning of this march, Martin Luther King Jr. was assassinated by a white man named James Earl Ray. The nation was devastated. The riots that ensued were difficult to quell and fueled the fires of rage and distrust for years to come. But, that is not what King would have wanted had he been alive — that much seems clear. King dreamed of a time that people of all colors, shapes, and sizes could live in harmony and not fear each other.

His legacy is strong to this day. He was able to make waves in a world that didn't even want him to exist. Now, thanks to the efforts of his ideological progeny, King will be remembered throughout American history. Through memorials that use his words to inspire people to this day, a federal holiday that respects his contributions to society, and innumerable works of arts reflecting his life, we can try to know what made Dr. King tick.

Above all, it is important to understand that there is no way he would now consider his work done. Even with an African American being capable of achieving the highest office, there is no end to the forces that try to keep the people of the United States divided. Recently, there has been an uptick in violence towards the African American community perpetrated by the very people tasked with keeping them safe.

The only thing to do is to try to understand exactly how King's message can be translated for a new generation. His life and the time he lived in was complicated, but his goals were clear:

And so even though we face the difficulties of today and tomorrow, I still have a dream. It is a dream deeply rooted in the American dream.

I have a dream that one day this nation will rise up and live out the true meaning of its creed: "We hold these truths to be self-evident, that all men are created equal."

I have a dream that one day on the red hills of Georgia, the sons of former slaves and the sons of former slave owners will be able to sit down together at the table of brotherhood.

I have a dream that one day even the state of Mississippi, a state sweltering with the heat of injustice, sweltering with the heat of oppression, will be transformed into an oasis of freedom and justice.

I have a dream that my four little children will one day live in a nation where they will not be judged by the color of their skin but by the content of their character.

I have a dream today!

Early Life

Martin Luther King Jr. was born on January 15th, 1929. He was the son of a reverend named Michael King and his mother was Alberta Williams King. He was the middle child of three, with an older sister and a younger brother. However, he was not born Martin Luther, his original name was Michael. His father was also Michael King originally. They would both change their name to Martin Luther when his father visited Germany in 1934. This decision was to honor Martin Luther, the legendary protestant reformer famous for the 95 Theses.

King would follow closely in his father's footsteps when it came to religion and politics. King Sr. was, also, born in Georgia—outside of Atlanta. He was a Baptist minister that spent his time lobbying for increased awareness for civil rights, especially with respect for the African Americans he represented. King Sr. was a member of the NAACP chapter of Atlanta and later became the leader of the entire chapter. He would encourage his son to participate in politics and get involved in the Civil Rights Movement.

King Sr., himself, was inspired by the Baptist ministers that he saw in his own parish. They were early champions of Civil Rights and inspired King Sr. to become a minister. He went away to gain his degree at Dillard University in New Orleans. During this time, he met his wife, Alberta, and began courting her. She was the daughter of another reverend that was close to his sister. He finally completed his degree at Morehouse School of Religion and married Alberta.

King Sr. settled down at the Ebenezer Baptist Church in Atlanta and began learning under the tutelage of his father-in-law. Once the elder reverend passed away, King Sr. replaced him as the leader of the congregation. It was no easy task for King Sr., as the great depression was in its full throes. The parish was threatened, but King Sr. raised the funds necessary to keep going. Once the smoke had cleared, he was able to claim full leadership of the parish and was a well-respected member of his community.

For four decades, he led the Ebenezer congregation as a stable and politically-active figurehead. It was during this time that he changed his and Michael Jr.'s names to match that of Martin Luther. He was able to gain support in both black and white communities with his brand of even-keeled, Christian-centered values. As King Jr. would later say:

"I guess the influence of my father also had a great deal to do with my going in the ministry. This is not to say that he ever spoke to me in terms of being a minister, but that my admiration for him was the great moving factor; He set forth a noble example that I didn't mind following."

King Sr. would even sometimes send his child out to work in the fields around Atlanta, to better understand the history of his American ancestors. The ancestry of the King family came from sharecroppers in the south. Sharecroppers were an exceptionally poor caste closely connected to slavery; many of them were, in fact, ex-slaves that found no better option than working on their old master's farm for slave wages.

It was due to these humble beginnings that King would spend the later part of his life putting together the "Poor People's Campaign". He believed, strongly influenced by his father, that his race was not only oppressed by law but also by forced poverty. Black men were discouraged from owning land and businesses by violence and unfair treatment, extending to their lack of real suffrage — eliminating their ability to work within the capitalist system to change their circumstances.

King, as a father, he would often take steps to help his son acclimate to the system of segregation and open racism that was very prevalent in Georgia. However, there would always be occasions of disrespect that would open King Jr.'s mind to what his father really thought:

Written by King Jr. in his autobiography:

"[After his father was asked to change seats with a white person in a shoe store] …this was the first time I had seen Dad so furious. That experience revealed to me at a very early age that my father had not adjusted to the system, and he played a great part in shaping my **conscience**. I still remember walking down the street beside him as he muttered, 'I don't care how long I have to live with this system, I will never accept it."

At another stage in his life, he was stopped by a police officer and referred to as a "boy" by the officer. King Sr. responded with barely concealed anger, "This is a boy, I'm a man; until you call me one, I will not listen to you."

There was nothing violent about it, but the defiance would stick with King Jr. for the rest of his life. He saw the power that his father could express, just by using his words. The white authority figures were not prepared to deal with a well-spoken black man who refused to be talked down to. Just the surprise alone would be enough to handle that situation.

King Sr. believed that the path forward for the African American community was rooted in a strong, politically active ministry. He worked to raise teacher salaries in the black community to equal those in white communities and was responsible for the destruction of many "Jim Crowe" laws in Georgia that kept African Americans from voting.

In a move that would later echo and inform his son's Montgomery bus boycott, King Sr. refused to use the public transport bus system after a brutal attack on an African American passenger that went unpunished.

He would continue to fight for his entire life, outliving his son and wife, who both died from gunshot wounds by assassins. King Sr. was there to receive the Presidential Medal of freedom with his son's widow, the absence of his wife and son was truly deafening.

However, King Jr. would enjoy a decent life in relation to other children in the African American community. He enjoyed education and moderate success, something his father made sure of. This would give King Jr. the tools he needed to become the great leader and orator he was.

King Jr.'s life was decidedly middle-class and he spent much of his time in school and church. He would become known for his participation in church choirs, just like his mother, who was an organist that toured with her talents and singer of high-caliber.

Much like a few other areas in the south at the time, the area in which King grew up in was home to some of the most successful African Americans in the country — known as one of the "Black Wall Streets". The other well known "Black Wall Street" was located in Tulsa, Oklahoma. It was burned to the ground in one of the largest race riots in the nation's history.

However, King Jr. was able to grow up safe in the love of his extended family and close community. There is still no way that he could have avoided the realities of a segregated south. King remembers back to when he was six and playing with a white child in the neighborhood.

One day, the white boy came over and told him that they were no longer allowed to play together, on the orders of his parents. A crestfallen King would surely remember that when he wrote his famous line, "one day...little black boys and black girls will be able to join hands with the little white boys and white girls as sisters and brothers."

King would suffer from depression and emotional issues for much of his early life. He would be able to conquer this issue as time went on, but it wasn't uncommon for young men of the time to have issues coping with the sometimes-hellish circumstances they were placed in.

When he was 12, King's maternal grandmother died from a heart attack. She passed quite unexpectedly while King was away. He had gone to a parade against the wishes of his parents and was in the middle of a defiant streak towards his parents. When he came back he found his family in mourning and King blamed himself. King fell from a two-story window soon after. Many consider that to be a failed suicide attempt.

He bounced back, however, and completely dominated his studies — skipping several grades in high school. School in the United

States, at the time, was heavily segregated. There was no way to ignore the disparity between the school systems, but still, King persisted. He was proficient in speaking and debating very early on.

One of the early cases of King Jr. having to come to grips with the racism of his time came on the bus ride back from King winning a speaking contest. King had performed admirably and was riding high; however, he was forced to stand on the bus to make room for other white passengers. King recalls that moment as the angriest he had ever been in his life. There was no victory that could not be ruined by prejudice.

He gained admission to Morehouse College at just 15, the same institution that his father and grandfather graduated from before becoming ministers. There was a shortage of applicants due to the war and King was an above average prospect, so he was able to enroll at such a young age.

King studied medicine and law and did not immediately have ambitions to become a preacher like his father. Again, however, the same forces that prompted his father to become involved in the ministry worked to great effect on King.

In those days, the community of African American churches was hotbeds of political ambition meant to bring about racial equality. King met a famous minister, Dr. Benjamin Mays, and he was convinced to both join the church and to fight for racial justice. Without either one of those influences, it is clear King would not be the man we think of today.

This change was good for more than just King's legacy; he was often distraught and unmotivated at that stage in his life. The first two years he spent in college were not used to their utmost capacity and it appeared his future may be in doubt. However, with the intervention of Dr. Mays, King was finally able to find the motivation to make a difference in people's lives and souls.

King Jr. had been skeptical of religion for much of his young life. He felt that there was an element of falsehood in the way that some members of the congregation expressed their faith so emotionally. King also questioned

many of the miraculous claims the bible
made, even going so far as rejecting the
Christian tenet that Jesus was resurrected
after his crucifixion. King says of the time,
"doubts began to spring forth
unrelentingly."

Still, as a young man in Morehouse, he
would eventually conclude that the bible had
many "profound truths" that he could no
longer deny. He would disappoint his father
greatly with his disinterest and defiance
towards Christianity in those days and that
was probably no small factor in his change of
heart.

Becoming Dr. King

Martin Luther King Jr. graduated Morehouse in 1948 with a degree in sociology and was able to join the Crozer Theological Seminary, again following in his father's footsteps. This time King came correct, he graduated as the valedictorian and enjoyed tenure as the president of the student body. It was during this time that King separated himself from the strict religion of his father and let his independence change the way he saw the world.

King partook in drinking beer and playing parlor games with his friends in a very traditional college fashion—something his father would look down on—especially at a seminary school. However, King would later renounce those ways, as he felt that it was his responsibility to shoulder the burdens of the African American race.

Still, King decided he would be a rational minister that spent his time spreading ideas and social justice as a service to humanity. He did not completely buy into the "fire and brimstone" ideology that his father espoused. His childhood was often spent in fear of his father, who was a traditional Christian disciplinarian. King would develop a much softer approach.

During his time at Crozer, King would fall in love with a white, German immigrant's daughter. She was the daughter of a woman who worked in the school cafeteria and was completely head-over-heels.

As you may know, King did not marry a white woman. He desired to marry her greatly, but was convinced by his friends and family that their life would be full of hardships. Both sides of the culture would refuse to accept King as a leader or important person if he was a part of an interracial marriage.

King broke off the relationship when his mother appeared to be in great pain at the idea. Tearfully, King conceded that nothing he could do would make the relationship work. It was said that King may never have truly moved on from that shock. It is hard to imagine a failed first love being harder than one that was ended prematurely because the world looked upon it with hatred and vilification.

King was able to heal enough to marry Coretta Scott in 1953 and they would have four children together over the next decade. She was, decidedly, less of a figure than she should have been in his life and would be relegated, by King, to stay at home as a mother in the traditional role — despite her efforts to support Civil Rights on her own.

King went on to complete his doctorate, serving as an assistant minister in the meantime. He would complete his thesis and earn his final degree in 1955. Years later, it would come to light that King may not have cited information correctly and he was posthumously accused of plagiarism. Nothing ever came of the charges.

From that point on, King's rise to the top of African American Civil Rights leadership was meteoric. After he graduated, he would become the pastor of Dexter Avenue Baptist Church in Montgomery Alabama. The stage was now set for one of the most important protests in American history.

King wasted no time following in his father's footsteps and using the pulpit as a method to affect social change. He became an executive member of the NAACP and was thus well positioned for the momentous change that was soon to follow.

The Beginning of the Civil Rights Movement

It may be hard to believe, but the King family became the center of a nationwide protest less than one year after moving to their new home: Montgomery, Alabama. By 1955 he accepted a role as one of the most important leaders in the national movement for equality.

To understand this situation correctly, it's important to understand the continuing and pronounced effect that Jim Crow laws were having in places like Alabama in the United States. These regulations were the last-ditch effort of white Democrats (those that were not complicit in the Confederacy and still retained power after the war) to curtail the equality of African Americans.

Jim Crow was a pejorative term given to a cartoonish depiction/understanding of African Americans. Essentially, laws were created to capitalize on the white public's misconceptions and racism towards black men and women. Typically, whenever Jim Crow was depicted, it was a picture of the incredibly racist "minstrel" style black man. Therefore, it can be assumed that there were actual laws on the books that could be literally described as "negro laws". Not only were these laws discriminatory, but they were insulting and deprecating.

There was little reasoning behind Jim Crow. It is hard to justify the systemic unfairness that was in effect all the way up to 1965, but the humiliation many racists felt after the emancipation of African Americans was surely a portion of the reason. This was the same time that spawned the KKK and other extreme, racist vigilante groups.

Essentially, knowing that all enslaved Africans were now free men capable of voting (as long as they were men), lawmakers would put social norms that were enforced by the previous power gap into actual, written laws. For example, there would be forced segregation of public facilities and services. That way, they could go on pretending that emancipation was not in effect — as long as there was some barrier between the races they could continue to consider themselves better.

This was often shrouded by the slogan, "separate but equal". However, it became a popular way to decrease the standing of African Americans in the public. Their facilities were significantly worse when it came to public works, education, and protection under the law. As stated earlier, King's father quit riding the busses in Georgia after a black man was assaulted publicly and nothing was done. This was common and accepted in those days, and some would say that has extended into the present.

Over half a century would pass before black Americans could vote to represent their interests. Not only were Jim Crow laws passed, entire state constitutions were changed to purge the voter rolls of African

Americans (and in some cases, poor whites as well). There was no way to change the process from the inside — African Americans couldn't even serve on juries.

The political capital in the south, where most black Americans lived at the time, was entirely held by the white-centered Democrats (which has very, very little in common with the modern-day party). The area was descried as the "solid South" because, once the voter rolls were purged of the Lincoln-following black Republican voters, there was no way the Republican Party could compete in the area.

Not only were the people of the South completely dominated by racist politics, but the violence that grew from that hate and

segreg[...]ering and unthinkable.
T[...]here entire towns
we[...]e a white posse was
formed to restore order". Murder was not
uncommon under the racist South and was
rarely punished.

This is when lynching became common as
well. The Tuskegee institute claims that
almost 5000 lynchings occurred during the
60+ years that Jim Crow laws were in effect.
In Georgia, where the King family was, their
586 lynchings led every state. This became a
practice that entire communities would
participate in. Hundreds to thousands of
people would gather, sometimes setting the
victims on fire, sometimes raping them,
sometimes removing body parts as
souvenirs, and always ensuring the death of

the victim. Hell was a real place on Earth and it still exists in the minds of some.

Years passed and black communities stood tall. Many were able to become prosperous and education kept improving along with the wealth of the community as a whole. That doesn't mean that they were safe, even as productive, healthy citizens. In fact, many times these communities were burned to the ground out of jealousy.

The wealthiest black community in the United States was found in the Greenwood district of Tulsa, Oklahoma. 35 blocks of the town were burned to the ground in 1921 after an attempted lynching. White men took to the sky in airplanes, dropping incendiary devices onto the homes and business of

African Americans. Over 300 people died in just one day in the heartland of the nation. 10,000 blacks lost their homes and millions of dollars (in today's dollar) were lost to the fire. Police and National Guardsmen were said to have joined in the mob, using machine guns against their own citizens.

It can be easy to understand why many black Americans were pushed to violence or extrajudicial activity themselves. Overall, it's very easy to understand the complete distrust of white institutions. This spirit is the birth of the King brand of civil disobedience. They were men of religion and Christianity. They abhorred violence but gave no respect to the institutions that used violence on them with regularity.

A small glimmer of hope was given to the African American community when Brown v. Board of Education was decided in 1954. A Supreme Court case was held to decide if it was possible to have separate facilities to educate children and still be equal under the law. The court decided 9-0 that it was impossible for two separate locations and institutions to be identical; therefore the law was inherently unequal.

The leaders of the Civil Rights Movement considered it a great victory. Schools would start to become integrated and districts were redrawn to alleviate the problems of inequality in the educational system. However, many states in the south refused to participate. In a famous scene, replicated humorously in the film Forrest Gump,

Governor George Wallace stood in front of the doors of the University of Alabama. He, and the Alabama National Guard, refused to allow two African American students to enter the building in order to register for classes. They were allowed to do so under the new Supreme Court ruling. However, Wallace ran under the platform "segregation now, segregation tomorrow, segregation forever".

Unfortunately for him, President Kennedy didn't appreciate National Guard resources being used to subvert the highest court in the land. He federalized the Guard in Alabama and forced Wallace's own soldiers to remove him from the doorway. This became known as the "Stand in the Schoolhouse Door".

Montgomery Bus Boycott

So, it came to pass that Alabama was the center of the nation's struggle for Civil Rights. It was just one year after Brown v. Board of Education. The strategy of the Civil Rights Leadership became "mass action". They were given enough protection from violence and murder (though that would soon change) that many were willing to put themselves out there and fight for their rights.

Boycotts began to work, beginning with a boycott of gas stations in Mississippi. African Americans began to use only black-owned banks, which would loan to Civil Rights groups that had been blackballed by white banks. Soon, the power of Civil Disobedience became apparent.

King and other leaders of the African American community in Montgomery had become fed up with the unequal, humiliating treatment many received on the public transportation system in the city. On busses, black women and children were forced, by law, to give up their seats for white men. In the same year of Rosa Parks, another woman named Claudette Colvin was arrested for not giving up her seat.

However, Claudette was an unwed mother. The male leadership decided that they would wait for a case that could not be easily dismantled by religious outrage and sexism (this interpretation is in the kindest light possible). So, they bided their time. Eventually, by the end of the year, another woman was arrested by the police for refusing to give up her bus seat, you may know her, and she was Rosa Parks.

Rosa was a respected member of the community and, by all accounts, a kind and righteous person. This was the moment they needed. However, it was not King and the men that sprang into action; rather it was Jo Ann Gibson Robinson and the Montgomery Women's Political Council that led the charge. They wrote and distributed 50,000+ leaflets that read:

"Another Negro woman has been arrested and thrown in jail because she refused to get up out of her seat on the bus for a white person to sit down. It is the second time since the Claudette Colbert [sic] case that a Negro woman has been arrested for the same thing. This has to be stopped...We are, therefore, asking every Negro to stay off the buses Monday in protest of the arrest and trial. Don't ride the buses to work, to town, to school, or anywhere on Monday. You can afford to stay out of school for one day if you have no other way to go except by bus. You can also afford to stay out of work for one day if you have no other way to go except by bus. You can also afford to stay out of town for one day. If you work, take a cab, or walk. But please, children and grown-ups don't ride the bus at all on Monday. Please stay off the buses Monday."

The leaflets worked and provided the necessary victory that would inspire others to continue the fight throughout the rest of the year. About 40,000 people boycotted the bus system for the first day — a massive portion of its total ridership, some say as much as 75%.

(As an interesting side note, there was no demand to end segregation. The protest simply demanded a more courteous ride and the ability to keep their seats if they had arrived first.)

The boycotts continued in Montgomery until a year later when the federal court system declared the law obsolete and forced desegregation on the bus system in Montgomery. They had won a victory that would have seemed impossible just a decade or two earlier. It was a victory they had not even necessarily expected for themselves, it lit a fire in communities around the nation.

King threw his full weight into the movement and founded the Montgomery Improvement Association that would go on to hold several more successful boycotts and undoubtedly changed the fortunes of thousand so African Americans in the community.

Once he was elected the president of the organization, he was given his first national platform and from that moment on, he was a popular national figure. He became known as the mastermind behind the success of the largest protest against segregation that had

occurred in the United States to that point —
all before the first year of his Montgomery
stay ended and before his 27th birthday.

However, that would not be the last of the
boycotts effects. The backlash from the white
community of Montgomery was substantial.
Over the year of the boycott, rifles were fired
into busses and violence increased
exponentially. A pregnant woman had both
of her legs broken by a bullet fired into a bus.
Churches were bombed, businesses and
homes attacked with explosives and bullets.

King was not immune; his home was the
location of a failed bombing that was
ultimately defused. However, that seemed to
be the final straw for local authorities. 7
members of the KKK were arrested and it

was then known that the police would, in fact, arrest racists who used violence.

However, through it all, King and his Montgomery Improvement Association remained committed to nonviolence. He had studied Mahatma Gandhi and concluded that public support would come to his side if people were forced to see nonviolent blacks suffer from the violent racism that existed in the South.

There is a lot of evidence that suggests this change was monumental when it came to helping the Civil Rights Movement. Pacifism as a guiding principal showed intelligence, education, and above all, a sterling commitment to the cause.

There are no short-term gains with pacifism; everything it teaches is about changing hearts and minds instead of winning victories of money or war. The North, in particular, would come to the aid of Civil Rights after centuries on doing nothing while the Southern powers did what they wanted to their African American constituents.

It's impossible to know how it felt being attacked every day and then going to your community and telling them to continue nonviolence. Malcolm X was especially critical of this strategy, as he had adopted the same mindset as many in Apartheid Africa, that is, guerilla warfare.

King would not falter, however. He wanted to bring his community together, as one piece. He believed that it was important the two cultures restored trust. He found that violence did nothing but sow those seeds of hate even deeper.

South Christian Leadership Conference

King was smart to capitalize on the fame and power that he was given after such a successful protest. He and other members of the fledgling Civil Rights Movement decided to create a new organization that would "redeem the soul" of America. Again, King shared the belief of his father that segregation and racism should be fought on the basis that it is an affront to God.

They wanted to separate all personal gain and victory from their goal of equality. Christians believe that every man and woman was created in the image of God. With that in mind, it seemed blasphemous that certain types of people would be held in a lower esteem.

So, the South Christian Leadership Conference was founded in 1957 with about 60 leaders of black congregations spread throughout the south. In the words of Martin Luther King Jr.:

"This conference is called because we have no moral choice, before God, but to delve deeper into the struggle — and to do so with greater reliance on non-violence and with greater unity, coordination, sharing and Christian understanding."

The initial meeting was held at King's home church of Ebenezer Baptist. They wanted to pull apart the resistance by appealing to the

Christian values of all the people involved, black or white. This could only be done with the use of nonviolence and they wanted to be at the forefront of the movement to steer the conversation in the direction that made sense to them.

They were not exactly an organization, in of itself, but they used their leadership skills to operate various organizations under their umbrella. Their first goal was to register as many African Americans to vote as they possibly could. According to King, "their chances for improvement rest on their ability to vote".

There was a large amount of resistance to their efforts by both white and black communities. Black communities wanted to wait and fight the battles in the courts, fearing white backlash. Obviously, white communities did not want to participate in changing the status quo.

But the real change here was the King-brand strategy that wanted to blend the forces of social justice and religion together. This was a concept interred directly from Martin Luther King Sr. to his son and is his greatest legacy. However, many churches were afraid to participate, rightly fearing retaliation and institutional prejudice.

Many of their efforts were successful, however. They were integral in creating what were known as "Citizenship Schools". They were institutions that specifically taught African Americans how to fill out the proper forms and registries that would allow them to be completely legal citizens.

By the peak of the effort, over 69,000 teachers were volunteering at Citizenship Schools in the southern United States. They became a great incubator for educated Civil Rights leaders of the future.

As they were pushing forward with education, the SCLC put more and more effort into supporting local protests and boycotts. The first was located in Albany, Georgia. Mass demonstrations were held and many were arrested, including King.

However, he was bailed out of jail just a few days later by the Chief of Police. King later said, "We had witnessed persons being kicked off lunch counter stools during the sit-ins, ejected from churches during the kneel-ins, and thrown into jail during the Freedom Rides. But for the first time, we witnessed being kicked out of jail."

The protests continued on for over a year. King was incarcerated a few times over that period, even being bailed out by Billy Graham at one point. However, the local government was unphased. At one stage in the protests, King was forced to cancel demonstrations, as they were getting more violent than he was comfortable with. Eventually, they were given assurances that their demands would be considered, but according to King, the agreements were dishonored almost immediately upon him leaving the city.

King would use the loss as a lesson, saying,

"The mistake I made there was to protest against segregation generally rather than against a single and distinct facet of it. Our protest was so vague that we got nothing, and the people were left very depressed and in despair. It would have been much better to have concentrated upon integrating the buses or the lunch counters. One victory of this kind would have been symbolic, would have galvanized support and boosted morale.... When we planned our strategy for Birmingham months later, we spent many hours assessing Albany and trying to learn from its errors. Our appraisals not only helped to make our subsequent tactics more effective, but revealed that Albany was far from an unqualified failure."

And so, the SCLC moved forward with their plans, more determined than ever to succeed in the face of unwilling opposition. The factors that had been in play for so long began to show their value by acting as a foil to the brutality that the Birmingham police showed the protestors.

King and the others learned that they must focus on specific issues in order to make permanent changes. This time it was to desegregate the downtown merchants of Birmingham, Alabama. They figured out that it was much easier to affect the existing order if their massive demonstrations focused on one weak point at a time.

Still, police commissioner "Bull" Connor found the impetus to violently oppose the protestors—a stark contrast to Albany, where nonviolent means were used almost exclusively. Connor thought he had eradicated the threat when he arrested King in a mass protest and local churches started to rebel against the idea of "outsiders" coming in and stirring up trouble.

King responded to a written statement by local clergymen with a letter now known as The Letter from Birmingham Jail. This was the 13th time that King had been jailed so far. His response is now regarded as a momentous affirmation of the cause he espoused:

"Several months ago, the affiliate here in Birmingham asked us to be on call to engage in a nonviolent direct-action program if such were deemed necessary. We readily consented, and when the hour came we lived up to our promise. So, I, along with several members of my staff, am here because I was invited here I am here because I have organizational ties here…One of the basic points in your statement is that the action that I and my associates have taken in Birmingham is untimely. … Frankly, I have yet to engage in a direct-action campaign that was "well timed" in the view of those who have not suffered unduly from the disease of segregation. For years now I have heard the word "Wait!" It rings in the ear of every Negro with piercing familiarity. This "Wait" has almost always meant "Never". I have almost reached the regrettable conclusion that the Negro's great stumbling block in his stride toward freedom is not the

White Citizen's Councilor or the Ku Klux Klanner, but the white moderate, who is more devoted to "order" than to justice; who prefers a negative peace which is the absence of tension to a positive peace which is the presence of justice; who constantly says: "I agree with you in the goal you seek, but I cannot agree with your methods of direct action"; who paternalistic-ally believes he can set the timetable for another man's freedom; who lives by a mythical concept of time and who constantly advises the Negro to wait for a "more convenient season."

National attention was always the goal of these protests, and in this way, the Birmingham campaign succeeded in a huge way. Almost 4000 school children left their classrooms and began to participate in the protests. In response, "Bull" Connor unleashed his police dogs and firehouses on the protesters--many of which were too young to be adults.

The national media elevated their coverage, eventually gaining the attention of President Kennedy. Just a week after the violence, a deal was made to desegregate and to refine hiring practices. This was King's second almost-miraculous victory over the forces of oppression.

However, King's greatest accomplishments were still yet to be seen. There was change in the air, and with every victory, the black community became emboldened. They were finally able to see the light at the end of the tunnel, there just might be a way to win against seemingly impossible odds.

March on Washington

With an even hand, you can say quite comfortably that 1963 might have been the most turbulent year in American history. President John F. Kennedy was assassinated. The FBI, at the behest of Robert Kennedy, began to wiretap Civil Rights leaders and those associated with them, including Dr. King. The culture of the United States was shifting rapidly. Gone were the days of conservative mainstream culture, with the arrival of the British Invasion and rock and roll—the U.S. would never be the same.

This was also the year of the Birmingham campaign. But, the most important Civil Rights demonstration was going on at the nation's capital, Washington D.C. This was a march many years in the making. Even in the 40's President Roosevelt issued an order that partially stemmed the tide of exclusionary practices used in government hiring and narrowly avoided a march.

However, this was a new day and the emotion needed to organize such a massive protest was available and raw. Violence was becoming more and more common in the South. This was shared by both sides, but the great majority of it was done by whites as backlash against the protestors.

So, planning began in late 1961 for a March on Washington. The planners had become unhappy with President John F. Kennedy and spared him no love when planning their approach. King, himself, described

Kennedy's views towards Civil Rights as "tokenism".

The main focus of the march was to improve joblessness amongst African Americans. The Civil Rights Movement would become unique in asking for federal assistance and championing socialist programs. This led to claims that the leadership was involved in Communism and led to a great deal of government suspicion.

However, King and the other groups involved did not believe in Communism. Rather, they saw the government give special treatment time and again to white-owned business and simply wanted an even playing field.

They would write as a part of the plan, "…integration in the fields of education, housing, transportation and public accommodations will be of limited extent and duration so long as fundamental economic inequality along racial lines persists."

The march came to be known as the March on Washington for Jobs and Freedom. The marchers received support from unions and others that wished to see a more egalitarian approach to government as well.

Eventually, the organizers were able to gather a "Big Six" of leaders of African American organizations. These men were: A. Phillip Randolph (the mastermind), James Farmer (Congress of Racial Equality), John

Lewis (Chairman of the Student Nonviolent Coordinating Committee and current U.S. senator), Roy Wilkins (NAACP), Whitney Young (National Urban League), and of course, Dr. King of the Southern Christian Leadership Conference.

This time, however, there was to be no sit-ins or boycotts. This was a show of complete solidarity among all who wanted to be a part of ending the racist regimes of American and change history. They didn't want to bring out the riot equipment; instead they felt as if their show of cooperation would be enough to make the difference they sought.

A few months before the planned demonstration, President Kennedy decided to give an address on Civil Rights in response to the increased violence throughout the country. This was just after George Wallace staged his famous door-blocking stunt and Kennedy was worried that his strong action against it might be misinterpreted.

Kennedy delivered the address brilliantly on television, capped off with this historic statement:

"We are confronted primarily with a moral issue. It is as old as the scriptures and is as clear as the American Constitution. The heart of the question is whether all Americans are to be afforded equal rights and equal opportunities, whether we are going to treat our fellow Americans as we want to be treated. If an American, because his skin is dark...cannot enjoy the full and free life which all of us want, then who among us would be content to have the color of his skin changed and stand in his place? Who among us would then be content with the counsels of patience and delay?"

King was enthralled with the speech, saying, "Can you believe that white man not only stepped up to the plate, he hit it over the fence!" This moment set the stage for the march, which was now to be a great moment of cooperation between the Civil Rights protestors and the American government. Kennedy would not make it out of the year alive.

As time went on, people began to pay attention to the march in greater detail.

Malcolm X, a longtime detractor of King's brand of protesting and a man who favored a more militant approach to change, called it a "farce on Washington". Kennedy and company began work on a bill that would try its best to echo the needs of the marchers. Opposition and support coalesced on all sides in advance.

The group itself disagreed about the way the march could be considered a success. Some wanted it to stand in direct opposition to Kennedy and the bill, while others still wanted it to support the newly supposed law. Either way, it was decided that their purpose would consist of these goals:

- Passage of meaningful civil rights legislation;

- Immediate elimination of school segregation;

- A program of public works, including job training, for the unemployed;

- A Federal law prohibiting discrimination in public or private hiring;

- A $2-an-hour minimum wage nationwide;

- Withholding Federal funds from programs that tolerate discrimination;

- Enforcement of the 14th Amendment to the Constitution by reducing

congressional representation from
States that disenfranchise citizens;

- A broadened Fair Labor Standards Act
  to currently excluded employment
  areas;

- Authority for the Attorney General to
  institute injunctive suits when
  constitutional rights are violated.

The march would also welcome white
supporters as a show of solidarity with any
that wanted to participate. Despite the FBI's
reference to the contrary, the march would
not accept any assistance from Communist-
related groups. It was common at the time
for Communist sympathies to be used as a
scapegoat in order to limit the impact of

certain liberal groups. Dr. King was not immune to this himself (he was not a Communist, but would later suppose that Capitalism had become obsolete when examined in relation to Civil Rights and the treatment of minorities).

The goal of the march was to summon at least 100,000 people to the reflecting pool at the base of the Lincoln Memorial, with their backs to the Washington Monument. The movement seemed to be gathering enough steam to achieve this response level. It certainly caught the attention of violent racists across the country; there were numerous bomb threats and attacks that were directly stated to be in opposition to the march. However, they persisted as they had done so many times before.

As the day came, the masses that appeared on the fields of Washington were enormous. A popular New York Times report gives a look into the reality of the situation:

The 260 demonstrators, of all ages, carried picnic baskets, water jugs, Bibles and a major weapon - their willingness to march, sing and pray in protest against discrimination. They gathered early this morning [August 27] in Birmingham's Kelly Ingram Park, where state troopers once [four months previous in May] used fire hoses and dog to put down their demonstrations. It was peaceful in the Birmingham Park as the marchers waited for the buses. The police, now part of a moderate city power structure, directed traffic around the square and did not interfere with the gathering... An old man commented on the 20-hour ride, which was bound to be less than comfortable: "You forget we Negroes have been riding buses all our lives. We don't have the money to fly in airplanes."

Everyone that participated had a different story, a different reason to be involved. And as the masses streamed forward, fear still persisted. However, people sang, they marched, they found ways to quell the fears inside of them and push ever forward towards, what they considered, their salvation.

President Kennedy remained true to his word. Although he levied nearly 6000 men to be used as security, there was the prevailing notion that nothing would be done unless their hand was forced by violence.

In a shocking turn of events, the massively expensive sound system that was procured for the event was sabotaged the day before. In a show of support, the United States Army Signal Corps stayed up all night to fix the system and it remained intact for the bulk of the march.

The entire nation was left watching as tensions came to a head on the day of. Televisions were left without a program besides those that covered the march. Thousands of reporters streamed to the capital, hoping to catch whatever greatness or evil came of it.

To the day that it was held, no one really knew how it would work out. However, the leaders of the Civil Rights Movement and Dr. King had faith that the people would come peacefully and powerfully. What happened next is pure history.

The Speech

The speech King gave that day is possibly the greatest in American history. He had prepared statements that went into detail about the plight of the African American. However, towards the end, affected by what he saw, something changed in him. He was struck by the massive success of the march and began to ad lib, using the stores of motivational knowledge available to him — after years of practice.

It is necessary, now, to dive into the speech and discuss its specifics. There may never be another time in which a speech would make such an impact on the world and, especially, America. King wrote his name in every textbook ever written by speaking the words that came from his heart. Here are the words that changed the world forever, shortened for your consumption:

Five score years ago, a great American, in whose symbolic shadow we stand today, signed the Emancipation Proclamation. This momentous decree came as a great beacon light of hope to millions of Negro slaves who had been seared in the flames of withering injustice. It came as a joyous daybreak to end the long night of their captivity.

But one hundred years later, the Negro still is not free. One hundred years later, the life of the Negro is still sadly crippled by the manacles of segregation and the chains of discrimination. One hundred years later, the Negro lives on a lonely island of poverty in the midst of a vast ocean of material prosperity. One hundred years later, the Negro is still languished in the corners of American society and finds himself an exile in his own land. And so, we've come here today to dramatize a shameful condition.

Here King started his speech by calling on the ghosts of America's past. He references Lincoln and the Emancipation proclamation as a great moment in American history. However, as he says, there is still not freedom for the African American. Notice the reference to poverty, a common theme to King's later speeches.

"In a sense, we've come to our nation's capital to cash a check. When the architects of our republic wrote the magnificent words of the Constitution and the Declaration of Independence, they were signing a promissory note to which every American was to fall heir. This note was a promise that all men, yes, black men as well as white men, would be guaranteed the "unalienable Rights" of "Life, Liberty and the pursuit of Happiness."

Here, King references the promises made to American citizens, given to them by the Constitution and our forefathers. He uses that promise and creates a metaphor of a "bad check". To him, those promises had not come true. Later, he would say (to laughter) that he refuses to believe that the "bank of justice is bankrupt".

"We have also come to this hallowed spot to remind America of the fierce urgency of Now. This is no time to engage in the luxury of cooling off or to take the tranquilizing drug of gradualism."

This statement was likely made in direct reference to critics within the African American community who accused him of being too soft. King throws out the idea of "gradualism" that was espoused by so many of his Civil Rights predecessors. To him, the time is now.

"It would be fatal for the nation to overlook the urgency of the moment. This sweltering summer of the Negro's legitimate discontent will not pass until there is an invigorating autumn of freedom and equality. Nineteen sixty-three is not an end, but a beginning. And those who hope that the Negro needed to blow off steam and will now be content will have a rude awakening if the nation returns to business as usual. And there will be neither rest nor tranquility in America until the Negro is granted his citizenship rights."

King stresses that this is not the culmination of anything. Rather, this is the beginning of a long struggle that will result in freedom and citizenship for all. Until that time comes, he refuses to stand down.

"But there is something that I must say to my people, who stand on the warm threshold which leads into the palace of justice: In the process of gaining our rightful place, we must not be guilty of wrongful deeds. Let us not seek to satisfy our thirst for freedom by drinking from the cup of bitterness and hatred. We must forever conduct our struggle on the high plane of dignity and discipline. We must not allow our creative protest to degenerate into physical violence. Again, and again, we must rise to the majestic heights of meeting physical force with soul force."

This is perhaps King's most lasting message. There would be no victory through bloodshed. The only way for true victory to come is for the hearts and minds of the people to be swayed. There is no military might that can triumph over the spirit of the free man. He would later say that he can see, by the presence of nearly 60,000 white people in the crowd, that whites had come to understand that "their freedom is inextricably bound to our freedom".

There are those who are asking the devotees of civil rights, "When will you be satisfied?" We can never be satisfied as long as the Negro is the victim of the unspeakable horrors of police brutality. We can never be satisfied as long as our bodies, heavy with the fatigue of travel, cannot gain lodging in the motels of the highways and the hotels of the cities. *We cannot be satisfied as long as the Negro's basic mobility is from a smaller ghetto to a larger one. We can never be satisfied as long as our children are stripped of their self-hood and robbed of their dignity by signs stating: "For Whites Only."* We cannot be satisfied as long as a Negro in

Mississippi cannot vote and a Negro in New York believes he has nothing for which to vote. No, no, we are not satisfied, and we will not be satisfied until "justice rolls down like waters, and righteousness like a mighty stream."

Here, King alludes to the basic goals of his movement. There is no victory until the injustices he speaks of can no longer be abided by the institutions designed to protect citizens. This is one of the more famous lines from the speech, especially the line that references the "negro mobility" from one ghetto to the next. King would, before his death spend much time helping bring awareness to the dangers of inequality.

"I have a dream that one day every valley shall be exalted, and every hill and mountain shall be made low, the rough places will be made plain, and the crooked places will be made straight…This is our hope, and this is the faith that I go back to the South with. With this faith, we will be able to hew out of the mountain of despair a stone of hope. With this faith, we will be able to transform the jangling discords of our nation into a beautiful symphony of brotherhood…And if America is to be a great nation, this must become true…

…And when this happens, and when we allow freedom ring, when we let it ring from every village and every hamlet, from every state and every city, we will be able to speed up that day when all of God's children, black men and white men, Jews and Gentiles, Protestants and Catholics, will be able to join hands and sing in the words of the old Negro spiritual:

Free at last! Free at last!

Thank God Almighty, we are free at last!

This is the end of King's speech. He expertly conjoins the old sayings and songs of American patriotism with the plight of the African American. After the smoke cleared from that era, experts and critics would come to see it as a masterclass in oration. King and the march would be seen as a success — and would be considered very impactful and dangerous to racial politics nationwide. However, that day, where over 200,000 marchers (twice the number that they expected) descended upon the capital may never be equaled when it comes to political impact.

Soon after, Congress passed the Civil Rights Act of 1964, which played a huge role in eliminating the legal basis of Jim Crow laws and legal segregation. Then, the next year, Congress passed the Voting Rights Act of 1965 that placed stringent protections on the voting rights of African Americans, particularly in the South.

King would go on to speak and march for a few years, but nothing could ever equal what happened on that day.

The Last Years

Though King had long been a part of the Civil Rights Movement, even he could not predict the events that would happen over the next few years. The government forces, led by J. Edgar Hoover of the FBI, continued to swarm on his every statement. Given the ability to tap his phones by Robert Kennedy, the FBI would try to blackmail King several times over his life in order to force him out of a leadership role. King persisted.

He began delivering an address entitled, "I Have Seen the Mountaintop" on a regular basis, moved by the progress that was made so swiftly since he had graduated and moved to Birmingham. He began to move his efforts towards more diverse pursuits, including opposition to the Vietnam War.

King felt obliged to speak on the behalf of the Vietcong and other nations that he considered to be under the yoke of imperialism. He would face vehement opposition for this, as it was seen as unfailingly unpatriotic. However, he persisted. He spoke these words during a famous speech titled, "Beyond Vietnam":

A true revolution of values will soon look uneasily on the glaring contrast of poverty and wealth. With righteous indignation, it will look across the seas and see individual capitalists of the West investing huge sums of money in Asia, Africa and South America, only to take the profits out with no concern for the social betterment of the countries, and say: "This is not just."

This echoes his largest sentiment in those years, that there should be a moral use of the resources that the nation had at its disposal. King championed the ideals of, what he called, a Democratic Socialism — recently made famous again by the campaign of Bernie Sanders.

He believed that there should be redistribution of wealth in the United States in order to combat the rigors of racism and the effect it had on the economic outlook of African American communities. One needs only to think back to the days of the Tulsa Race Riots to understand his thinking behind this.

Many accused him of Communism for this reason and it has been supposed that his eventual assassination was at the behest of anti-communist forces, rather than racial upheaval.

The year before his death, King conspired to create another march; one he thought would equal or exceed the power of the March for Jobs and Freedom. He called this the "Poor People's Campaign". He called for an "economic Bill of Rights" that would shield the poor and disenfranchised from the brutality of Capitalism. He was one of the early supporters of a guaranteed basic income.

The idea behind a guaranteed income is that it evens the playing field for all involved in the Capitalist society — allowing groups that were otherwise not profitable to exist with greater efficiency. This may have crossed the line with many of his supporters as it is, to this day, considered a radically liberal proposal. Still, many liberal tech magnates have come out in favor of it in recent times — nearly 50 years after his death.

Unfortunately, every story about Dr. King has to end with his assassination. The years following his march contained many threats and attempts at his life. But none were successful until James Earl Ray.

Ray was a convicted felon who had been jailed for multiple crimes, some of them violent. His life was one spent on the run, even as a child. He underwent a very early version of rhinoplasty and spent some time in Mexico as a fledgling pornographer.

Above all, Ray was a racist. He strongly supported the campaign of George Wallace, again the same man who stood in the door of the University of Alabama. He agreed with Wallace's segregationist ideals and worked for the campaign for months. Eventually, Ray left for Atlanta and purchased a rifle. The FBI contends that there was a map of Atlanta, with King's residence circled, left in his room when they searched it after the shooting. Ray read an article that stated King would be in Memphis on April 3rd. Ray decided to drive up with his rifle, intending to do harm.

Ray would later say that he thought that his prison sentence would be shortened once George Wallace was the president, though that day never came for either of them.

After King delivered an address at a rally on April 4th, 1968, he went to his favorite motel in the area and spent time with friends in family in his room. Around early evening, a shot was heard ringing out of the courtyard. King fell with a fatal shot to the jaw that traveled to his shoulder.

King was frantically delivered to the nearest hospital and given emergency surgery. He did not survive. It has been said that his heart was aged almost twice the amount that it should have been for a 39-year-old man. This was likely due to a genetic heart deformity that leads to the death of his father and one of his siblings. However, his supporters believed that it was due to the stress put on him by being a leader in Civil Rights.

Ray would confess to the crime and plead guilty, at the behest of his lawyer, so he would not receive the death penalty. However, Ray would later recant his confession and start a life-long struggle to get a retrial on the basis that he was simply a pawn in a larger conspiracy to assassinate King.

There has been little credence given to the idea the Ray was not the shooter. His fingerprints were found on the weapon that fired the bullet which killed King. He also possessed the motive and means to travel to do so. He was a lifelong criminal with nothing to lose that specifically hated the idea of desegregated society.

To his credit, however unpalatable, the King family believes him. They think that he was a part of a plot that involved the FBI and J. Edgar Hoover—much the same as the thinking behind the JFK conspiracy.

Regardless of why someone would kill King, he often was afraid of it happening, his death only strengthened his legacy. A crowd gathered that day to listen to him speak. He gave his "Mountaintop" address and seemed to be oddly calm. It was odd because, that same day, his plane had to be unloaded due to a bomb threat against him. He spoke of this in the last speech he gave:

…And then I got to Memphis. And some began to say the threats, or talk about the threats that were out. What would happen to me from some of our sick white brothers?

Well, I don't know what will happen now. We've got some difficult days ahead. But it doesn't matter with me now. Because I've been to the mountaintop And I don't mind. Like anybody, I would like to live a long life. Longevity has its place. But I'm not concerned about that now. I just want to do God's will. And He's allowed me to go up to the mountain. And I've looked over. And I've seen the Promised Land; I may not get there with you. But I want you to know tonight, that we, as a people, will get to the Promised Land. So, I'm happy, tonight. I'm not worried about anything. I'm not fearing any man. Mine eyes have seen the glory of the coming of the Lord."

He will be forever missed.